CW00497802

Super]

Species appropriate nutrition for guinea pigs

A guide to adequate guinea pig food and
to reduce your costs

ALINA DARIA

Content

For Leopold, Lexi and Lana.

And for all other guinea pigs out there!

Prologue

It can be surprising how many people feed their pets contrary to their species-appropriate diet. Of course, this does not happen intentionally, but mostly out of inexperience. You love your little rascals and only want the best for them.

Accordingly, you obtain information, get advice and study various guides. Unfortunately – or rather, to the detriment of the animals – a huge amount of false information is being disseminated, both on the internet and partly also in relevant guidebooks.

But at least the employees in the pet shop must know about appropriate nutrition and be able to offer sensible advice, right? No. Not at all. The pet store wants to sell its alien food, just as it wants to sell the cute guinea pig or the sweet puppy – just to get replenishments from dubious breeders who treat the animals as pure products and raise them under completely unworthy conditions. But that's a different topic.

It's not a drama if you've been feeding your animals wrongly, or at least partially wrongly. There are simply too many dubious sources. I have been holding rodents for almost thirty years – whether it was hamsters, guinea pigs or rabbits (or all at the same time). I shudder to think about what mistakes I made at the beginning. Well, I stuck to what was written in renowned guidebooks at the time. In these, however, it was also recommended to keep guinea pigs in a small cage from the pet shop. In addition, it was stated that it would not be a problem keeping them solitary. Well, it was almost thirty years ago. Fortunately, we know better today!

Before we begin: Product reviews are the basis for the success of authors. Therefore, I would be grateful for feedback on this book in the form of a review. Please post your review on the platform where you purchased this book. You will also help future readers and collect a few points on the karma account! Thanks a lot.

So, how do you feed a guinea pig appropriately? We now want to get to the bottom of this question!

Leopold wonders who knocked on his door...

Is there a fresh delivery of grass?!

The physiology of the guinea pig

Hopefully, we all already know that guinea pigs are neither carnivores nor omnivores. Guinea pigs are pure herbivores (plant eaters)!

The guinea pig originally comes from South America. It came to Europe by ship over the sea. The squeak typical of guinea *pigs* was reminiscent of young piglets. However, they are not related to pigs.

The climate in South America, home of the guinea pig, is very warm and often relatively humid. Accordingly, the guinea pig mainly feeds on grasses, wild herbs, and leaves. Logical, right?

Grass is, so to speak, the basis of every meal and the main food of guinea pigs. It is therefore not surprising that hay should be the main component of the diet and that it is recommended that hay be provided to guinea pigs around the clock. Because what is hay? Hay is simply dried grass, mostly enriched with dried wild herbs.

The guinea pig's teeth are aimed at crushing and grinding the food. Guinea pigs can move their teeth sideways and thus grind their food before swallowing it – just like humans. This is another difference to the carnivore, because the carnivore (lion, cat, etc.) has fangs and pointed molars to disassemble its prey and swallow it in large pieces almost without chewing.

That is why it is so important that guinea pigs have enough
to do with chewing their food. Have you ever eaten grass?
If not, give it a try. Honestly. Just a few straws. Grass is so
rich in crude fibers that you feel like you have to chew it
forever until you can get it down. This constant chewing is
incredibly important for the preservation of guinea pig
molars. If guinea pigs don't have enough to chew, dental
problems can quickly arise! The constant chewing means
that the upper and lower molars grind each other.

If you are already a guinea pig owner (and are not just about
to make your first acquisition), you have certainly noticed
how often guinea pigs eat – and how **much** they eat
accordingly. That is why it is so important not to humanise
guinea pigs; while people usually eat two to four times a day
and do "number two" on average one to two times a day,

guinea pigs eat between 30 and 80 (!) times a day and poop (what feels like) constantly. And that's super important!

Why? Because guinea pigs have a stuffed stomach. As the name suggests, this means that food must always be "stuffed" from above so that "something comes out" below. This principle is also different from that of humans, so once again it is important not to humanise guinea pigs.

The human digestive tract works continuously and gets along well with two or three large meals a day without coming to a standstill. The human digestive system pushes the food on to the next station on its own until the unusable waste is finally excreted. People can even fast for a few weeks without starving and without stressing the digestive system. Fasting can be extremely healthy for humans - but for guinea pigs even a few hours without food can be fatal.

Guinea pigs have to keep eating food to keep the digestive tract going. The food is pushed from the stomach into the small intestine. From there it continues into the cecum. In the cecum, the nutrients and vitamins are used (that's why the "cecum-poop" is often so healthy!) And the 'waste' is excreted towards the end.

If you feed your guinea pigs properly, you don't have to worry about them gaining weight and becoming fat. Animals that live in the wild do not get fat. Only humans get fat because, unfortunately, our species is shoveling more and more garbage into their bodies. The only animals that

are or become fat are some pets – and this is solely due to
the poor feeding methods of the owners. Or have you ever
seen a fat animal in nature? Nope. Logical, huh?

Lexi likes to produce a lot of poops.

Vitamin C

Guinea pigs cannot produce vitamin C themselves – by the
way, neither can humans. Therefore, both humans and
guinea pigs have to get their vitamin C externally through
food. However, the addition of vitamin C drops is usually
not necessary. It is much healthier to take in vitamin C from
fresh food. We'll discuss a little later which fresh feed is a
good supplier of vitamin C.

First time feeding

Please keep in mind that every new food has to be fed slowly and in moderation first. Especially if you have mainly fed your guinea pigs with dry food (i.e. with hay and conventional pellets or dry food containing cereals/grains), you should switch to fresh food very slowly and carefully monitor your guinea pigs to be able to determine whether they are getting used to the new food at the right pace.

Do not cut out dry food overnight but reduce it for about a week or two until you finally no longer offer dry food at all (the exception is hay – the piggies should always have hay available!). At the beginning, every new food should only be offered in small quantities daily, such as a fingernail-sized piece or a handful of leaves, so that the small stomachs and tiny intestines can get used to everything new. Otherwise, digestion problems could arise.

Where can I find species appropriate food?

Not everyone is lucky enough to have a forest nearby where all sorts of grasses, tree species and wild herbs grow. And that is ok. You don't need to offer your guinea pigs every kind of wild plant if you simply don't have the opportunity.

However, take a look around or find out where you can find suitable trees, grasses, and herbs in your area. If in doubt, first ask your city or council whether you can pick food for your guinea pigs at the respective location. Usually this is not a problem. For safety's sake, you may emphasize that you are not a breeder so that the council does not think that your food collection will eventually become too much.

It would of course be ideal if you had a forest in the immediate vicinity. In the forest you will find many different types of trees and large meadows with a variety of herbs and grasses.

Otherwise you can usually find what you're looking for here:

- In the garden of friends and relatives (they will be happy to help you)

- At nearby farmers (ask permission beforehand, of course)

- On the side of the road (ideally on streets that are not too busy because of the exhaust gases; if you collect from the side of the road, I recommend that you wash the food well)

- In parks

- At lakes and ponds

- On dirt roads

It is easy to collect food on dirt roads.

Especially if you want to pick from friends, relatives and / or farmers, you should definitely inquire whether poisons (such as rat poison) are used there.

As a rule, it is not necessary to wash leaves, grasses, and wild herbs before feeding. In the wild, animals also eat their food unwashed, so this is not a problem. Many guinea pig keepers also report that their guinea pigs do not touch dirty food (which was contaminated, for example, by dog urine or similar) anyway.

Keep in mind that guinea pigs have a much better olfactory organ than humans. Usually the guinea pigs can select very well and pick the best pieces from a mountain of food. Therefore, some food will always be left and not eaten.

You also don't have to worry if it was raining and the grasses, herbs and leaves are wet. You can feed them wet – again with the same reason: In nature, animals also eat rain-soaked feed.

If allowed, you can collect guinea pig food in some parks.

A lake or a pond is very suitable for foraging.

Hay

Hay must be available to your guinea pigs all around the clock. Hay is dried grass, usually enriched with dried wild herbs such as dandelions and the like. Hay has an extremely high proportion of raw fibers. These are low in calories but must be chewed well and thoroughly. This is particularly important for tooth abrasion and for intact digestion.

In perfect circumstances, guinea pigs would feed on meadow 24 hours a day, 7 days a week, 365 days a year – especially on grass. However, this is not possible in every country. Especially in Europe and North America, it is often impossible to offer fresh grass to the animals all year round. In winter you may find a few barren stubs of grass. Therefore, hay serves as a substitute food and is indispensable.

It is often wrongly assumed that guinea pigs have to eat hard food so that their teeth are rubbed off. This is where most of the mistakes start. Unfortunately, many guinea pigs are often offered dried hard bread or nibble sticks. That is suboptimal. At first glance, it may seem logical that hard bread is good for tooth abrasion, but the opposite is the case.

The bread soaks through the saliva in the mouth and does not need to be chewed for a long time. The food is swallowed quickly. In addition, bread – or cereals/grains in general – saturates the guinea pigs for a very long time, which is also counterproductive. Guinea pigs should eat small portions regularly. Ideally, they always chew food that needs to be chewed for a long time – and that is above all hay when there is no fresh grass available!

Otherwise, the guinea pig's teeth will grow longer, and this can cause serious problems. This is different than in humans. At worst, the guinea pig will refuse food at some point if the teeth hinder feeding, the vet will have to grind the teeth, or there will be even worse tooth and digestive problems.

Many guinea pigs that get fresh herbs, fresh leaves, and fresh grass from spring to autumn are usually not too interested in hay. When guinea pigs have a choice between hay and fresh grass, they usually choose fresh grass. And that is perfectly fine and a good thing.

Nevertheless, hay should also be offered when fresh grass is offered at the same time – just as water from a bowl should always be offered, even if the guinea pigs obtain most of their water requirements from fresh food.

You should also note that guinea pigs usually pick the best straws in the hay. It is normal for guinea pigs not to eat all of the hay provided. They should be able to choose the most valuable stalks and leave the rest behind.

Therefore, you should provide new hay every day, even if the old hay from the previous day has not been (completely) eaten. Under no circumstances should you "force" the animals to finish everything before you give them new food.

There are over two hundred different types of grass, but very few are used as feed. Usually between two and twelve different types of grass are used to produce hay. Examples are ryegrass, knotty grass or meadow panicle.

Hay should always be stored dry. It must not come into contact with moisture. It should also be stored in a dark place – for example, a wooden box, cardboard boxes or cloth bags are ideal for storage, as the hay can still "breathe". Plastic packaging is therefore unsuitable.

Grass

The absolute and undisputed favourite food of guinea pigs:
simple grass! All types of grass are suitable for forage and
are extremely important for tooth abrasion and digestion.

Please do not feed grass which had been cut with a lawn
mower. Grass cut by a mower is being fermented extremely
quickly and might cause bellyache. It is best to simply pluck
or tear the grass by hand or to cut it off with (garden)
scissors.

To emphasize it again: don't worry if the grass is wet. You can still feed it. In the wild, guinea pigs always feed on grass when it rains. This means that even more liquid is absorbed than if only dry grass were eaten.

However, you shouldn't leave wet grass (or grass in general) too long as it eventually will ferment. It's best to make sure you feed the grass the same day or the next day. If I had extremely little time, I fed grass easily two days later. However, you should make sure that the grass has not yet started to ferment and that it still looks fresh and crisp.

Wild Herbs

While you can find different grasses almost everywhere, the search for wild herbs is sometimes a little more complicated.

Depending on where you live, you will be able to find more or less different types of wild herbs near you. The more different wild herbs you can offer, the better it is of course – also because guinea pigs are specialists in selecting exactly what they need.

Some wild herbs can be found almost everywhere like sand by the sea. I would argue that almost everyone can find at least dandelions and nettles around them – and of course daisies. You may be lucky enough to have a forest or other green space nearby. Often you don't even pay attention to which plants you are surrounded by every day. You may also have friends or family with a garden where wild herbs grow.

We start with the classics below!

Dandelions

Dandelions are definitely one of my favorite herbs – and more importantly, one of my guinea pigs' favourite herbs. Experience has shown that the leaves of the dandelion are particularly popular. However, you can feed the entire plant, including the stem and flower.

Dandelion contains a lot of provitamin A and also vitamin C (about 67,778 µg per 100 grams). Since guinea pigs cannot produce vitamin C themselves, a dandelion is a perfect supplier of this vitamin.

It is often criticised that dandelions contain too much calcium and that this can promote calcium deposits, which can lead to urinary and kidney stones and bladder sludge. However, this only applies if the guinea pig is fed inappropriately.

Usually, when guinea pigs are properly fed grass, herbs and vegetables, such diseases cannot occur because too much calcium is simply excreted by the guinea pig. With a species-appropriate diet, the guinea pig takes in enough water to simply flush out excess calcium.

Dandelions with flowers and leaves

Therefore, don't be surprised if you find whitish pee in the
enclosure of your guinea pigs – this is only a sign that
calcium has been flushed out, so there is usually no need to
worry.

It can only be problematic if the guinea pig takes in too
much dry food, especially pellets. Pellets are not species-
appropriate at all and do not belong in the tummy of the
guinea pig. Because where in nature would a guinea pig find
and eat pellets? Right, nowhere. Salt lickstones are also
completely unnecessary since salt is known to draw water
from the body.

Dandelions are also diuretic. So, they ensure that the body
is always flushed out well.

Nettles

I must admit, not all of you will be thrilled to read about
nettles in this guide. Everyone knows them, everyone
knows what they look like, and most of all everyone knows
how painful their touch can be.

Nevertheless, the nettle is one of the healthiest herbs of all
times. Like the dandelion, it is diuretic and also cleanses the
blood. The nettle also contains a lot of vitamin C (up to
333,000 µg per 100 grams) and also important minerals such
as iron and magnesium. In addition, nettles have a large
amount of vitamin B1, but also vitamins E, A and various
other B vitamins.

Nettles

Nettles "burn" due to their small hairs and can cause wheals on the skin. But that doesn't necessarily need to happen – if you cut off the plant at the bottom of the stem and then pull it upwards through your hand, the tips of the hairs break off and they no longer burn.

It is best to do this with gloves. In addition, you should pull the entire nettle several times (I recommend three or four times) to make sure that all hairs have been caught. If you burn yourself, don't panic – nothing will happen. Incidentally, guinea pigs cannot "burn themselves" on nettles anyway.

However, guinea pigs don't prefer them all fresh, but slightly withered. Therefore, you can leave them for a few hours before you offer them to your piggies.

Daisies

When guinea pigs eat daisies, it not only looks incredibly adorable, but is also extremely healthy! Valuable bitter substances and flavonoids can be found in daisies. These have an antioxidant effect and contribute to a strong immune system. In addition, the daisy also comes up with magnesium, iron, potassium and vitamins A, C and E. The entire plant can be fed, especially the flower is very suitable. Daisies are also digestive, blood cleansing and metabolism-stimulating – so they are ideal for guinea pig nutrition.

Daisies in a meadow

Clover

Shamrocks

Fortunately, clover is quite easy to recognise because the leaves are very characteristic and easy to remember. In addition, everyone knows that a four-leaf clover is said to bring good luck – the appearance of the clover is very well known.

Red clover with its typical pink flower

Clover belongs to the family of the flowering plants. Both
the leaves and the flowers can be used or eaten and fed.
Potassium, calcium, magnesium, vitamin C, vitamin B1,
vitamin B3, flavonoids and many other valuable ingredients
can be found in clover. Accordingly, it is an optimal food
for guinea pigs.

Ribwort plantain

The plantain leaves

Ribwort plantain is known as a natural antibiotic and is commonly considered a medicinal plant. There are almost two hundred different types of plantain, with the ribwort being undoubtedly the most common and the easiest to find in most areas. The whole plant is healthy and can be fed, with the leaves being the most popular.

Plantain, for example, contains a lot of vitamin C, zinc, B vitamins, silica, and potassium. It is antibacterial, blood cleansing and can inhibit inflammation. Thus, plantain is perfectly suitable for guinea pig feeding.

Furthermore, plantain has an excellent antibiotic effect and
can therefore help with infections of the throat and lungs,
should a guinea pig catch a cold despite all caution. Colds in
guinea pigs are to be taken very seriously and should
definitely be looked after by a veterinarian, since otherwise
(unfortunately often fatal) pneumonia could develop very
quickly.

The typical flowering of the plantain

Chamomile

The chamomile flowers

Most people probably know chamomile primarily in the form of chamomile tea. But behind the tea there is a beautiful, delicious and healing plant that is also popular with guinea pigs.

Chamomile is extremely helpful with stomach aches. If digestion is thrown off track, chamomile can help and alleviate it very well. Chamomile grows from May to September and is mainly found in fallow land or in fields in Europe.

Not only can the chamomile flower provide a good remedy for indigestion and stomachaches, but it also has an anti-inflammatory, antibacterial and antioxidant effect due to the flavonoids it contains.

Bedstraw

Meadow bedstraw

There are many different types of bedstraw. The most common and easiest to find are the meadow bedstraw and the burdock bedstraw. Burdock bedstraw is very easy to recognise as it is quite sticky.

Bedstraw can be found all over the world. It has a diuretic effect and is therefore often used as a natural remedy. It also contains valuable flavonoids and essential oils. The flavonoids help to build a strong immune system and work extremely well against bacteria and viruses.

Bedstraw can also be extremely cancer-cell-inhibiting, which is also important for the small guinea pig bodies.

Ground ivy

Ground ivy with leaves and flowers

Ground ivy belongs to the labiate family. It contains
valuable bitter substances that can support digestion and
metabolism perfectly.

Ground ivy also contains valuable vitamin C, which guinea
pigs need to obtain from food. Ground ivy also supplies, for
example, valuable essential oils, tannins that have an
antibacterial and anti-inflammatory effect, silica and
potassium. Ground ivy is most often found on meadows, in
gardens or in embankments. They like humid climates.

Ground ivy should be mixed with other herbs and grass
before given to the guinea pigs. It should only be offered in
small quantities and not as a primary feed.

Treating all edible wild herbs in detail would go beyond the scope of this guide. Perhaps I will write a detailed guide later on wild herbs exclusively. There are simply (luckily) too many herbs that can easily be fed to guinea pigs.

Nevertheless, at the end of this chapter I list a few more wild herbs that you can offer your animals and that can be found frequently.

If you are not sure what type of plant you are picking, I recommend using an app for plant identification! At the beginning I used such an app every day to make sure that I correctly identified the plants. I recommend the "Plantnet" app with a clear conscience.

Important: this is not advertising. I am not paid to recommend this app. The recommendation is based solely on my extremely good experience with the app. In the app, you can take a photo of the respective plant and then receive suggestions as to which plant it can be. This is not always clear. It's best to photograph the entire plant with leaves and flowers (if applicable).

If you are still not sure, let the plant stand and ask a specialist first. You are also welcome to send me a photo of the plant and I will be happy to help you determine it!

Other wild herbs that can be eaten by guinea pigs and are popular with many guinea pigs:

- *Amaranth*

- *Dock*

- *White plantain*

- *Watercress*

- *Thistles (guinea pigs don't get hurt from their thorns)*

- *Veronica*

- *Cinquefoil*

- *Lady's mantle*

- *Goutweed*

- *St John's wort*

- *Garlic mustard*

- *Marguerite*

- *Broadleaf plantain*

- *Rapeseed*

- *Marigold*

- *Sorrel*

- *Yarrow*

- *Celandine*

- *Chickweed*

- *Cranesbill / geranium*

- *Deadnettle*

- *Thyme*

- *Bird vetch*

Please do not feed the following (poisonous) plants (non-exclusive list):

- *Aloe*
- *Arum*
- *Christmas rose*
- *Ivy*
- *Monkshood*
- *Fern*
- *Foxglove*
- *Laburnum*
- *Autumn crocus / Meadow saffron (Deadly for piggies and humans!)*
- *Lilies*
- *Lily of the Valley (Deadly for piggies and humans!)*
- *Oleander*
- *Delphinium*
- *Deadly nightshade / belladonna*
- *Solanum*

If in doubt, please always research whether a certain plant is edible for guinea pigs. Humans and animals often differ, and this can also vary from species to species.

Trees: Leaves and Branches

In addition to grass, herbs and leafy vegetables, the leaves of trees can also be fed – sometimes guinea pigs like even dried leaves.

The most popular among my guinea pigs are the leaves of beech, birch, oak, and hazel. There are different genera here, all of which can be fed.

Oak

The greatest feature of oak is that it stimulates digestion extremely well and is effective against diarrhea, for example. We already know how important it is to keep an eye on your

guinea pigs' digestion. The oak can really get the digestion
going again and regulate the bowel activities well.

Oak

Birch

Like the nettle and the dandelion, the birch has a diuretic effect. In addition, the birch can have anti-inflammatory effects.

Birch

Beech

The beech is also extremely popular with guinea pigs. That is a good thing indeed since it can help against cold symptoms such as runny nose, but also against increased temperature. It is a natural cold remedy, so to speak. In my experience, the most popular is the hornbeam.

Beech

Hazel

Compared to the trees described above, the hazel has extremely soft leaves. They feel quite tender. You can find the hazel in red (although the color looks more purple) and green. You can feed both types well. The hazel works well for diseases of the internal organs, especially in relation to the liver and bile.

Hazel

Leaves and branches of other trees you can feed to your guinea pigs:

- *Apple tree*

- *Apricot tree*

- *Bamboo*

- *Pear tree*

- *Blackberry tree*

- *Fig tree*

- *Spruce*

- *Ginkgo*

- *Blueberry*

- *Raspberry*

- *Currant tree*

- *Pine*

- *Cherry tree*

- *Basswood*

- *Mirabelle*

- *Poplar*

- *Peach tree*

- *Plum tree*

- *Gooseberry*

- *Fir trees*

- *Willow*

- *Hawthorn*

Under no circumstances should you feed the following tree species (toxic!):

- *Boxwood*

- *Yew*

- *Maikoa / Angel's trumpet*

- *Lucky bamboo (is not a real bamboo)*

- *Elderberry*

- *Laurel*

- *Magnolia*

- *Guelder rose / viburnum*

- *Castor / Palm of Christ*

Lettuce

Leafy vegetables are perfectly fine for guinea pigs. Therefore, lettuce can also be safely fed to guinea pigs and should represent a large part of their food, especially if meadow feeding is not possible or not possible every day.

However, there are some big differences between the different types of lettuce. Some varieties are richer in nutrients than others and offer greater value for guinea pig feeding.

Bitter lettuce are by far the most suitable for feeding your guinea pigs. The bitter substances contained therein are healthy for humans and guinea pigs. While people often do not like a bitter taste, they often try to cover the bitterness through sweeter dressings and the like. However, guinea pigs seem to really love bitter foods. No wonder the extremely bitter dandelion leaves are my guinea pigs' favourite!

Endive

A typical winter lettuce is, for example, the endive lettuce. This is very practical if in winter, no meadow or only a few grasses and herbs can be fed.

In addition to the endive, the bitter lettuce that can be fed well include the radicchio, frisée and chicory. My guinea pigs like radicchio best! Of course, this can vary from guinea pig to guinea pig. It's best to try out whether your guinea pigs like all types of bitter lettuce or prefer certain varieties.

Radicchio

The bitter substances in the lettuce listed above are extremely good for digestion (super important for guinea pigs!), biliary function and the liver. Bitter substances can also have an analgesic and anti-inflammatory effect. Bitter lettuce is still extraordinarily rich in vitamins and contain, for example, vitamin C and various B vitamins. But important minerals such as potassium can also be provided by bitter salads.

In addition, very healthy and tasty lettuce for guinea pigs are also arugula (although arugula is actually a cabbage!), romana, lollo rosso and lamb's lettuce.

Arugula

Lamb's lettuce

Most other types of lettuce are not recommended for guinea pig feeding or should not be fed too often. These include iceberg lettuce and butterhead lettuce. These types of lettuce have an extremely low mineral content and contain too much nitrate.

Vegetable greens free from the supermarket and weekly market

Anyone who visits the supermarket or weekly market will notice that people usually leave or throw away the parts of a vegetable that are a delicacy for guinea pigs and can be fed to them often.

Who of you has ever eaten carrot greens? Or kohlrabi leaves (also called turnip cabbage)? Or cauliflower leaves? Probably only a few.

Exactly these greens are extremely suitable as food for guinea pigs. Most guinea pigs especially love kohlrabi leaves! It is of course very convenient that people do not normally eat these parts of the vegetables.

In many supermarkets and from the weekly market, you can often take veggie greens with you free of charge, otherwise it would be thrown away anyway. You even take a little bit of work off the supermarket or the retailer by using the vegetable greens in another way.

Of course, you should first ask whether take-away of veggie greens is permitted. I have various supermarkets in my area that are happy for me to take the vegetable greens for my guinea pigs. Once you have received their OK, you do not usually have to ask again each time but can simply pick up the green or take it with you when shopping. So, you not only ensure that these foods are still used and do not become "waste", but it is also great for your wallet!

I can particularly recommend the following vegetable greens:

- Kohlrabi leaves

- Carrot green

- Cauliflower leaves

- Radish leaves

- Celery leaves

Cabbage

Cabbage is ideal for winter feeding your guinea pigs! We have already discussed which grasses and herbs you can find outside in winter. However, this will most likely not be enough for complete feeding, which is perfectly fine.

The main component of your winter feeding should be bitter lettuce and various types of cabbage. It is often erroneously claimed that cabbage bloats and therefore causes gassing.

This is only the case under three circumstances, all of which should be avoided anyway, even if no cabbage would be fed:

1. If, in addition to the cabbage, pellets or conventional dry food are fed as well. Pellets and dry food from the pet shop are, as previously discussed, completely unnecessary and unnatural. If you give your guinea pigs dry food / pellets and want to stop, you should wait about two weeks before offering them cabbage.

2. If you don't feed the cabbage slowly. If the changes in feeding are too rapid, indigestion can always occur because the guinea pig's digestion did not have enough time to adapt to the new food. Therefore, the following also applies to the cabbage: Please feed slowly over several days. For example, on the first day you can offer a fingernail-sized piece, the next day a finger-sized piece, the next day a handful, etc. Of course, provided your guinea pigs respond well to the new food.

3. If your guinea pig doesn't get enough exercise. Exercise is particularly important for healthy digestive activity. Incidentally, this is also the case with humans.

There are some types of cabbage that have a fairly high content of high-molecular carbohydrates and should therefore only be fed little. These cabbages can actually promote gasification if they are eaten in excessive quantities and/or if a certain guinea pig has a sensitive digestive system.

These cabbages also have a high proportion of water-binding fiber, which is another reason why they should be consumed in moderation. These are Brussels sprouts, red cabbage, white cabbage, and savoy cabbage.

Apart from that, all other types of cabbage are very well tolerated. In my experience, the most popular are kohlrabi and kale. Cauliflower, Chinese cabbage, pak choi and broccoli are also popular.

Other Vegetables

Many other vegetables can optimally complement your guinea pigs' menu. How many vegetables you feed in addition depends on how much and how often you can and want to feed from a meadow (i.e. fresh grass and fresh wild herbs and leaves). From spring to autumn, many guinea pig keepers feed their animals exclusively from fresh green from nature.

Of course, whether this is possible for you depends on many factors – for example, where you live, how much time you have, etc. Some people find a lot of grass in their environment and maybe three to four different feedable herbs, but that would be just not varied enough to cover all needs and to offer a relatively wide selection.

Therefore, we now want to take a closer look at some easily digestible, common vegetables that are valuable for guinea pigs.

Fennel

Fennel is one of the best remedies for stomach aches. Maybe you already got fennel tea for a tummy ache as a child and you still reach for this tea as an adult if something hurts in the stomach or abdomen or needs to be brought back into balance.

Fennel works just as well in guinea pigs. The taste of fennel is very well received by guinea pigs, the lower and inner part of the fennel bulb is often particularly popular. Despite the very good and easily digestible properties, fennel should not be the main feed, but can also be served daily as a side dish.

Fennel

Peppers

All types of pepper are suitable as feed. It took me a bit of time to find out which part of the pepper guinea pigs like best: the inside! Guinea pigs and humans complement each other wonderfully again. While humans cut out the white inner parts of the peppers and remove the seeds, this is the tastiest part of this vegetable for guinea pigs. Peppers also serve as a great source of vitamin C.

However, be careful not to feed the green stalk of the peppers. This is not digestible because it contains a lot of solanine. My guinea pigs seem to know this intuitively, or it just doesn't taste good, in any case the stalk (or the tiny rest of the stalk) is always nibbled to the end and then left behind.

Tomatoes

All tomato varieties are suitable as feed. Ideally, however, you shouldn't feed tomatoes too often or only offer them in small quantities, as they are relatively acidic. This can favour lip grind. If a piggy has lip grind, you should generally avoid all acidic vegetables and fruits. Please also make sure that you do not feed the green of the tomato. This can be toxic due to the high content of solanine. Apart from that, the tomato is completely unproblematic and can be offered from time to time.

Carrots

Carrots belong to the bulbous vegetables and are extremely popular with most guinea pigs. However, since they have a relatively high calorie count for guinea pigs, carrots should not make up a particularly large part of the food but should better serve as a side dish or snack.

By the way: Do not be surprised if your guinea pigs bite off pieces of the carrot and spit them out immediately. Sometimes they spread these pieces all over the place. It took me a while to figure out why my guinea pigs do this: sometimes they don't like the skin of the carrot and just nibble it off to get to the (sweeter) core. On other days, they eat the whole carrot. That varies from the variety of the carrot and probably also from guinea pig to guinea pig.

Cucumber

For many, cucumbers are the typical standard food for
guinea pigs. Cucumbers are not the best food for the small
guinea pig body, because they supply almost exclusively
water and hardly any nutrients.

Many guinea pigs only like the skin of the cucumber and
leave the rest behind. Therefore, you should of course take
special care that the cucumbers are of organic quality since
the skins are often sprayed.

In summer, cucumbers can be used as a cool down, for
example in a shallow water bath, from which the guinea pigs
can fish out the cucumber slices. Especially on very hot
days, cucumber feeding can ensure that your guinea pigs
consume enough fluids in order to prevent dehydration.

The following types of vegetables are not suitable as guinea pig food:

- *Avocados*

- *Beans*

- *Mushrooms*

- *Chilli / Jalapenos*

- *Potatoes*

- *Horseradish*

- *Olives*

- *Radishes*

- *Rhubarb*

- *Onions*

Treats

Yes, we should feed our animals species-appropriately and
healthily. Lots of hay, grass, wild herbs, leaves, branches,
lettuce, cabbage ... But seriously, do you treat yourself to a
piece (or a bar) of chocolate now and then? A bag of crisps?

Most people 'treat' themselves at least every now and then,
so I think it is quite legitimate to allow our animals their
treats too! After all, eating not only satisfies human beings,
but it also makes piggies happy.

The absolute favourites of my guinea pigs are sunflower
seeds (without the shell!) and pea flakes.

Sunflower seeds are rich in vitamins E, B1, B3, B6, magnesium, zinc, and iron. In addition, they are a pure wholefood, so they occur in nature in exactly this form. Of course, guinea pigs are not nut, seed and grain eaters. But as a treat in between, sunflower seeds do very well and are also healthy. Furthermore, they work very well against dry skin.

At the same time, however, sunflower seeds are very fatty and contain almost fifty per cent fats – therefore, in excess, they can make an animal chubby. Sunflower seeds should never be offered unlimited in a bowl or the like but should ideally be fed by hand in moderation.

By hand feeding you strengthen the bond and trust between your animals and yourself. At the same time, it also promotes communication. As a rule, my guinea pigs only get their treats when they got up on their back feet. A little bit of exercise, in addition to running around and popcorning, is not a bad thing either.

At the beginning, I simply held a sunflower seed over the nose of the piggies so that they had to stand on their feet if they wanted to get it. If they did not understand this, I first held the core to their nose and then slowly raised my hand so that they followed my hand and got up.

Sunflower seeds

In addition to the workout bit, this of course also looks extremely cute. It also helps my guinea pigs to communicate with me. We all know the loud squeaking noises when we rustle with a bag or open the refrigerator. Our animals are conditioned to the fact that there is most likely food that will either be unpacked from a bag or that comes from the refrigerator – so they start squeaking loudly in anticipation. Perhaps also because they think we are making something for ourselves – and they want to point out that they want something too.

Now my animals can also tell me unequivocally if they want a treat – then they come closer to me and stand on their hind feet. For me this is the sign: "Hello mommy, look how nicely I can stand up, now give me a treat!"

When I have friends visiting and they are at the enclosure, my animals sometimes come to my friends, look at them and stand up on their hind legs. Logically, my friends don't understand this sign and just think it's cute. Then I have to explain that the animal is communicating with them and asking for a treat. And that will be rewarded!

Another very popular treat is pea flakes. Pea flakes consist entirely of dried peas, which are then pressed into flakes. Strictly speaking, this is not a whole food because the peas have been processed. However, because pea flakes consist only of dried peas and the only processing method was drying and rolling, we let them count as whole food.

When you consider that guinea pigs normally eat foods that are high in water and therefore supply fewer calories, it is logical that pea flakes are calorie bombs for a small guinea pig. Therefore, they should only be offered in moderation as something "special" and only fed from the hand.

For guinea pigs, pea flakes are what chocolate is for humans – only that peas provide a lot of vitamins and minerals (vitamins A, C, E, K, B vitamins, folic acid, magnesium, calcium, zinc, iron). Pea flakes can be offered as a snack but not unlimited, only in moderation from the hand. Treats should never be offered in bulk or in small bowls. Also, the anticipation of the animal is maintained every time.

Other popular and possible treats for guinea pigs include:

- Blueberries

- Apple pieces

- Blackberries

- Pieces of banana

- Raspberries

- Grapes (white / green / red)

- Cranberries

- Pumpkin seeds

- Linseed

- Cumin

Lana loves her pea flakes.

Pellets / Dry Food

The most widespread mistake that is made when it comes to guinea pigs is the feeding of pellets or dry food containing grain/cereals. If you've fed your guinea pigs with pellets so far, don't blame yourself. You can get this from so many places, especially bad guides and pet stores.

Unfortunately, such a diet is completely alien and causes many diseases, especially digestive diseases and dental problems, as there is not enough tooth abrasion.

One might think that the teeth would be rubbed off on the hard pellets. Unfortunately, this is not the case because the pellets soften quickly because of the saliva and are not chewed very well either.

The best thing for tooth abrasion is grass (or the long-lasting variant: hay). On grass and hay, the piggies chew for an exceedingly long time, which is extremely important for maintaining healthy teeth. The teeth then rub each other off.

Furthermore, pellets and cereal-containing dry food swell a lot. This is not at all good for a sensitive stomach like that of a guinea pig.

You might be able to guess what most guinea pigs die from prematurely – exactly, dental problems and/or digestive problems. And both are very strongly influenced by the (alien) diet.

So why don't guinea pigs need dry food? The domestic guinea pig as we know it originates from the Tschudi/Montane guinea pig, which comes from South America. This guinea pig prefers to live in mountainous regions, especially in the Andes.

Do you know how the climate is there and what is growing there? Exactly, there are mainly grasslands and forests. And what are piggies eating there? Grasses and wild herbs or wild plants and leaves. No pellets with cereals and grains.

The guinea pig is able to process and digest cereals and grains. But that doesn't mean that it is physiologically designed to do that, as it is an herbivore. Such a diet is alien and makes the guinea pigs sick in the long run and presumably also fat.

It's like with humans: Humans are not designed to eat meat. Of course, humans can process and digest meat. However, this does not mean that they were created physiologically to do so. Humans are fruit eaters (which includes legumes, vegetables, whole grains, nuts and the like) according to their physiology, while guinea pigs are herbivores according to their physiology.

The basis of the herbivore diet consists of grasses and leaves such as herbs, tree leaves and leafy vegetables or lettuce or leafy cabbage. If you eat a different diet, sooner or later you will get sick. This applies to humans as well as to guinea pigs.

So, let's take a look at the list of ingredients from some of the big feed producers for guinea pigs. I prefer not to give names. Most feed mixes are put together in a similar way anyway.

1. Cereals/grains (including wheat, oats, corn, barley) → You can actually stop reading there. None of this belongs in a guinea pig's stomach!

2. Vegetable by-products → That can mean anything and nothing. "By-products" is usually a nicer word for "waste". No joke. For industry, this is just waste. In order to use it profitably, it is mixed into the guinea pig feed.

3. Vegetables → Well, congratulations. Better a little dried vegetables than none, right?

4. Oils and fats → Why? Just why? Should we prefer to dip the dandelion in oil for our guinea pigs before we feed it as well? It is completely unnecessary and unhealthy to feed oil to a guinea pig. It does not even have to be vegetable fats – it can also be animal fats. So, some producers even turn the guinea pig into a carnivore!

The situation is similar for the second feed manufacturer. The main ingredient is grain/cereal again. This is followed by the vegetable by-products (i.e. the waste) and then dried fruits and vegetables. At least. And then we're back to oils and fats. So, it runs seamlessly from manufacturer to manufacturer. So please keep your hands off of pellets. Your guinea pigs will thank you.

The worst thing about dry food, however, is that it is _**dry**_ (as the name suggests). Guinea pigs need _**hydrated**_ food, like grasses, herbs, and leafy vegetables. A guinea pig that is properly fed will hardly drink water because it already consumes so much _**water through food.**_

Nevertheless, you should always offer water in a bowl as well. I advise against drinking bottles because this does not correspond to the nature of the animal. Almost all animals drink in nature from streams and rivers with a lowered head. Water from the bowl comes closest to that. Logical, right?

Change of Diet

It is very important that every change in food should and must be done very slowly! The human body is more robust than the guinea pig's body and can cope with a new kind of food almost immediately. Guinea pigs, on the other hand, have to get used to new food slowly.

Especially guinea pigs, which have been given dry food and are now to be switched to grass, herbs and leafy greens, need their time.

The intestinal flora has to get used to everything new. It is therefore recommended that the dry food be slowly discontinued within one to two weeks.

So, less dry food is fed every day. At the same time, the volume of fresh food is steadily increasing. For example, if your guinea pigs have never eaten fresh grass, give them a few stalks on the first day, a little more on the second day, a handful on the third day and so on. After about a week or two of feeding, the guinea pig can eat unlimited fresh food.

Otherwise, digestive problems such as gas or diarrhea may occur. This seems paradoxical at first, because fresh feed is so healthy and should not cause any diseases. And that is correct. However, the guinea pig's digestive tract is so sensitive that it cannot cope with changes that are too rapid.

This is also important for winter. Experience has shown that in winter you cannot feed as much (or no) grass and herbs from outside as in spring, summer and even in autumn.

However, even in winter you can still find grass and stubborn herbs such as dandelions, daisies, or ribwort here and there.

Therefore, at best, you should still feed small amounts of grass and herbs in winter if you have the opportunity to not completely wean your guinea pigs.

If your living situation does not allow this, this is fine – only then you have to feed everything very slowly again in spring, because the digestion of your guinea pigs has forgotten the previous foods and has to get used to them again.

Epilogue

I hope I have helped you with this guide. As we have found, the guinea pig is an incredibly special being and is vastly different from human beings. It is therefore important to know the needs of this species so that it can be optimally cared for.

If you have any further questions, don't hesitate to drop me an email. You can find my email address in the legal notice.

In conclusion, dear reader: Product reviews are the basis for the success of authors. Therefore, I would be very grateful for feedback on this book in the form of a review. Let me know in your review how you liked the book. You will also help future readers and collect a few points on the karma account! Thanks a lot.

Have fun with your guinea pigs, all the best and stay healthy and happy!

Legal Notice

Title: Super Poopers – Species appropriate nutrition for
guinea pigs – A guide to adequate guinea pig food and to
reduce your costs

Author: Alina Daria Djavidrad

Contact: Wiesenstr. 6, 45964 Gladbeck, Germany

Email: info@simple-logic.net

Web: https://www.simple-logic.net

© 2020 Alina Daria Djavidrad

1st edition (2020)

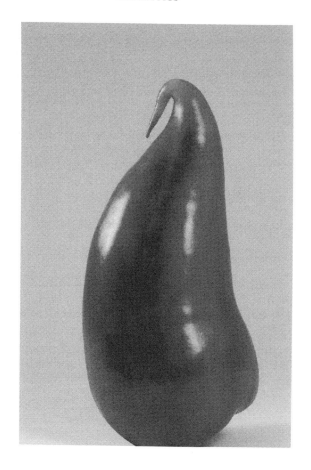

Printed in Great Britain
by Amazon